THE STORM

Peter Oswald

THE STORM

OR 'THE HOWLER'

an Appalling Mistranslation by Peter Oswald
of a Roman Comedy by Plautus

OBERON BOOKS
LONDON

First published in this adaptation in 2005 by Oberon Books Ltd
521 Caledonian Road, London N7 9RH
Tel: 020 7607 3637 / Fax: 020 7607 3629
e-mail: oberon.books@btinternet.com
www.oberonbooks.com

A catalogue record for this book is available from the British
Library.

ISBN: 1 84002 585 9

Cover image: Graphic Thought Facility

Printed in Great Britain by Antony Rowe Ltd, Chippenham.

Characters in the Play

The **Weather**

Sun and **Rain**, his helpers

Sceparnio, a slave

Daemones, his master

Plesidippus, a young man in love

Palaestra, a prostitute

Ampelisca, a prostitute

Labrax, their pimp

Charmides, his helper

Ptolemocratia, priestess of Venus

Venus

The play takes place in ancient Greece

The Storm was first performed at Shakespeare's Globe on 30 July 2005 with the following cast:

Sun, Liz Collier

Ptolemocratia, Fiona Creese

Sceparnio, James Garnon

Plesidippus, Alex Hassell

Charmides, Edward Hogg

Palaestra, Emma Lowndes

Daemones / Labrax / Weather, Mark Rylance

Ampelisca, Jodie Whittaker

Rain / Venus, Siân Williams

Musicians, Phil Hopkins (MD), Irita Kutchmy, Dai Pritchard

Master of Play, Tim Carroll

Master of Design, Laura Hopkins

Master of Music / Composer, Claire van Kampen

Master of Dance, Siân Williams

Master of the Words, Giles Block

Master of Movement, Glynn MacDonald

Master of Voice, Stewart Pearce

Assistant to the Master of Play, Natalie Abrahami

Assistant to the Master of Design, Gaëlle Lindingre

First Part

Enter SUN and RAIN.

Sun Ladies and gentlemen, would you please switch off

Rain All anachronisms

Sun As this play is set in Roman times and the classical
atmosphere would be ruined

Rain By your ringtones.

Sun Groundlings, please keep your feet on the ground

Rain Not your bums

Sun Or you'll be sold as slaves

Rain To the people in the galleries.

Both Thank you!

Exeunt. Enter the WEATHER.

Weather Qui gentes omnes mariaque et terras monet, eius
cum civis –

Ha! Had you worried there for a moment! I am the
weather. You can call me Clement. It won't make me
any better. I'm racist. I hate the English. That's not
true actually. I hate everybody. What I really hate is
coverings. Raincoats, that's bad enough, but umbrellas,
that really is raising two fingers. Roofs! What's wrong
with me? Let me in, I've got something to say! That's
why I rattle on the door, that's why I stamp on the
ceiling! Come out and get wet! Only then will you
understand me!

Look out! There's something happening
Along this foaming coast,

7

Whose headlands are hands grappling
With a great watery ghost

This cottage on the cliff
Is the dwelling of Daemones,
A man who gave his life
To the heaping up of monies,

Till one day he decided
To give it all away;
Scrabbling for lucre he derided
On that illuminous day;

Then just when his last coin was gliding
Out of its ivory chest,
A gang of traffickers came riding
Out of the whispering west,

Snatched his daughter in broad daylight
Off of the garden swing,
And galloped away into the greylight
Of the cold evening.

The ransom they demanded, well,
The father he could not pay,
They've dragged her through ten types of hell
For twenty years and a day.

She was three years old when they took her away,
A screaming bundle of loot,
Now in Cyrene, round the next bay,
She's working as a prostitute,

As fate would have it! A rich young man
Wants her to be his permanent lover –
He's made a down payment to the pimp; the plan
Is that she will be handed over

Here, at the shrine of Venus, but
The pimp has split with the deposit,

And with the girl, in a speedboat.
The sea's as calm as a water closet –

Which is when I, with lightning in my mind,
Suck in the wide sky, blast it out again,
Ink-black, pole-cold. They are far out upon
A sea-saw surface in a nest of matchsticks,
And when I flex the sinews of the wind
And lash the horses of the water on,
It is a foolish soul whose navigation
Is to unrighteous harbours! He'll not reach them!

Exit blowing up a storm. Enter SCEPARNIO.

Sceparnio Bloody terrible night. Windy? I peeped out at
one point, saw a shadowy figure gliding towards me over
the garden. A bear? A ghost? Our neighbour? The garden
shed. I shut the door again. A whole new vista has opened
up upwards. Yes I was lying there as luck would have it
in the attic where I am honoured and privileged to take
my rest. I never knew I'd miss that roof so much. I had no
idea it meant so much to me that roof but I can tell you
I was heartbroken when it went. I thought we really had
something going, me and the roof, but one click of the
wind's fingers and it was off. Lonely? I suddenly felt what
it is like for the earth to be the only inhabited planet in the
cosmos. Probably. Yes, there's not much out there in the
way of company. Pluto, basically a sphere of ice, whichever
way you look at it. Venus – sounds great but if you answer
her phone booth ad, turns out to be a green lump lashed by
storms of sulphuric acid. If we can think of the solar system
as a kind of party, and I think we can, the earth is the only
one there that's even trying. It must feel like it's wandered
into a zombie barndance. But I'm proud of that sea. Look
at it! That's what I call kicking up a fuss. Never lonely by
the sea, if you're seaborn, as I am. That's my sea, that is,
Mare Sceparnicum. Not a lot of people know that. No one
in fact. It's our secret.

Enter PLESIDIPPUS.

Plesidippus Nothing!

Sceparnio I beg your pardon?

Plesidippus Nobody! Agh!

Sceparnio Can I help?

Plesidippus Nobody! Nothing! Nothing! Nobody!

Sceparnio I don't find this very flattering quite frankly.

Plesidippus Where have you taken her, you wolf, you blemish?
    Only the proud cliffs chesting down the ocean,
    Only the gulls, pale mountaineers despairing
    Of the wind's sheerness, only this old ruin,
    And the heart-empty temple of the goddess.
    Not a soul. No one! Where I had expected
    To meet my love and make her mine forever!

Sceparnio Hello!

Plesidippus Ambushed by emptiness! As if a man
    Should climb a golden ladder to the moon,
    Expecting the celestial, and find there
    Only the dust of the cremated gods.

Sceparnio And a great big smiling all too human being!

Plesidippus Perhaps this slave can tell me some small thing.
    Unless his tongue has been cut out. But then,
    Would it be kind to make him strain his mind?
    Aha, the master!

Enter DAEMONES, looking at the non-existent roof.

Daemones What?

Sceparnio I know.

Daemones What, what, what?

Sceparnio I know, I know, I know.

Daemones How? How?

Sceparnio I don't know. I don't know.

Daemones Bloody hell!

Sceparnio Bloody, bloody hell!

Daemones Ha!

Sceparnio Haha!

Plesidippus Sir –

Daemones Hang on a minute.

Plesidippus Quite.

Daemones Well well well.

Sceparnio Tut tut tut.

Daemones Damn you Sceparnio, you let my roof blow off!

They both burst out laughing for a long time, pointing at the roof.

To think! Ha! To think! I once lived in the most expensive house in Greece, the villa Croesus! I could have roofed this house with one of the doormats of that one! Good riddance.

Plesidippus Sir, I do not know your name –

Daemones Daemones.

Plesidippus Mr Daemones.

Daemones Sir, I do not know your name.

Plesidippus Plesidippus.

Daemones Mr Plesidippus, we live a long way from anywhere else. How and why you have got here I can't guess. That way for miles and miles, crags and combes and combes and crags – same that way. We have to make do as best we can for laughs.

Plesidippus Have you finished?

Daemones For the moment.

Plesidippus Why have I come here? Is that what you wonder?
Well I have come to find my love, my bride,
The woman I have paid good money for.

Sceparnio How much?

Plesidippus Mr Daemones?

He indicates that he is asking permission to hit SCEPARNIO.

Daemones No point. Too far gone.

Plesidippus Mr Daemones, will you tell me please,
Has there been any shadow-eater here,
Horrible slicked-back fag-ash coloured hair,
Fragrance of public toilets in the springtime;
Thin. Kind of pressed into himself, a vampire,
A weak black hole incapable of sucking
Anything in but twilight, whole stars never,
Though on his arm you'd see a stolen beam
Of sunlight in the image of a woman,
Butterfly in a spider's web, gold coin
In a thief's fist or Venus under Vulcan?

Sceparnio Stop!

Plesidippus What?

Sceparnio You nearly trod on the weak part of the cliff there, where it's about to collapse. Close one!

Plesidippus That would have been the end of me!

Sceparnio That would have been the end of the play. We need that for the denouement. So how much did you pay for her? Roughly.

Plesidippus Mr Daemones, why do you not answer?

Sceparnio How can he, when you go mentioning things?

DAEMONES sits with his head in his hands.

Plesidippus What have I mentioned?

Sceparnio You'll have to deal with me now. You won't get another word out of him for six weeks minimum.

Plesidippus What have I mentioned?

Sceparnio There you go, trying to tempt *me* to mention it! Oh no, I'm not one of you mentioners.

Plesidippus I only ask a very simple question!

Sceparnio Simple! You take us for simple folk, don't you, simple country folk whom you can mention anything you like to! Well we have feelings too. We are complicated. You say one thing to us, it reminds us of other things. It sets off vibrations. How much did your wife cost? Ball park figure.

Plesidippus How dare you!

Sceparnio How dare you, he says! When he's just – Well I will tell you, just so you know. Are you listening master?

Daemones No.

Sceparnio I will tell you what you have said. His daughter was kidnapped when she was three.

Plesidippus Ah.

Sceparnio So don't talk to him about paying for woman!

Plesidippus All right, but have you seen –

Sceparnio How much?

Plesidippus Fifteen grand.

Sceparnio What? I cost more than that!

Plesidippus I doubt it.

Sceparnio Fifteen grand? Are there bits missing?

Plesidippus Shut up.

Sceparnio Is she? Faulty digestive system. You should
have got them to knock off a bit more for that.

Plesidippus I know where you live.

Sceparnio Look, you need what I know.

Plesidippus I hope you know something.

Sceparnio I know this – we've got a whole shedful of
wives out the back better looking than yours going
for ten, twelve, fourteen. We've got everything from
your bog-standard basically charmless but does-the-job
four grand right up to your pukka fifteen and a half
flexible with foreign languages and, for an extra Archer
– humour.

Plesidippus No you haven't. And you have not seen my
wife!

Sceparnio Oh no? I might have done.

Plesidippus You could not speak like that if you had seen
The one I love! The swollen springtide moon
Is like an eyepatch on the night, the dawn
A schoolboy's blush compared to her my friend!

Sceparnio (*Aside.*) This is the kind of incurable romantic
who loves his inflatable woman for her personality.

Daemones Oh! Oh!

Plesidippus Mr Daemones, would you intervene?

Daemones You must get thatching, my dear boy, and mend
  The rip that lets our dreams out and lets in
  The rain the rain the bloody bloody rain.

Plesidippus Mr Daemones, if you would prevent
  A loss like yours from happening again –

Daemones You never can have seen such weather, friend.
  Did you come out to see the way the breakers
  Still thunder though the vigour of the wind
  Has passed inland? The ones in front conform
  To the momentum of the ones behind
  That were stirred up far out. So grief keeps on
  After its cause is spent – above, dead calm:
  But on the beach the storm's a long time dying.

Plesidippus No sir, I came here on an assignation,
  To meet my bride, here at the shrine of Venus,
  And take her over from the man who owns her.

Sceparnio A cheap woman sir, but dear to this gentleman.

Plesidippus She is not cheap, and nor should you imagine
  She would be! She is beautiful, and clever,
  She can play anything on the piano.

Sceparnio Ping pong?

Daemones Who is her owner?

Plesidippus A man called Labrax.

Sceparnio Labrax?

Plesidippus You know him?

Sceparnio A famous overpricer of women!

Plesidippus Sir, you do not beat your slave enough! Please!

Sceparnio And you paid him a deposit I expect.

Plesidippus Yes!

Sceparnio And he said I'll meet you at the shrine of
Venus tomorrow morning, with the girl.

Plesidippus Yes! Yes!

Sceparnio But –

It all finally dawns on PLESIDIPPUS.

Daemones You may hit him now by all means.

PLESIDIPPUS sits with his head in his hands.

Plesidippus My life!

Sceparnio He'll have escaped with her by sea.

Plesidippus Last night! Oh then the rocks have got her surely,
Or else the dogfish. I have never seen –

Daemones No, no, of course not.

Plesidippus   Even in a dream –
Another who could – there was something – something –

SCEPARNIO notices something.

Sceparnio That's a strange two-legged whale evolving out
of the sea.

The others don't hear him.

Plesidippus This is disastrous.

Daemones   Yes, of course it is.

Plesidippus My father gave me a lump sum, to help me
Start up a business.

Daemones   Business, business, business!

Plesidippus Now I have lost it on the one I love –
Or most of it. She was worth all of it!

Sceparnio Two of them clinging together like drunks
in the foam of the ocean! Or one four-legged beast?

Woops! One goes down and takes the other one with
him! The first one gets up. So does the second one.
Then – oh dear, the second one knocks the first one
down. Or was it the first one? Sir, we are being invaded
– sort of –

Plesidippus What could I do? The woman they intended
To be my wife, is a petite green Venus
Flytrap! A kind of witty well bred pony!
And she sucks laughter out of every lung
Except for mine. And when I saw the other,
Dressed as herself, out of the music school
Descending like Persephone arising!…

Sceparnio So you said bog off to your parents and fixed
yourself up with a deranged marriage.

Plesidippus The gold pupated in my purse and floated,
Butterfly-bright, into the net of daylight.

Sceparnio But look, who's that?

Plesidippus What? A survivor of the night! What shipwreck
Has cast them up? Is it my love? Oh sweetheart!

Sceparnio Which of those two rather sad looking middle-
aged men is your sweetheart? The one vomiting or the
one being vomited on?

Plesidippus Labrax! The pimp who split with my deposit!
What has he done with my heart's moonlight? Lost her
At sea and all my father's money with her!
Well I will throw him back into the ocean!

Exit.

Sceparnio Good luck.

Daemones A mere apprentice of distress, newbound
To the grey trade, not yet attuned like I am,
Hearing the thunder of a thousand doors
Closing on hope down fortune's corridors.

The bank of Human Gladness
Has crashed, gone out of business.
The school of ancient wisdom
Has been burned down by arson,
The temple of divine delight
Is showing cowboy films tonight,
And as for Happy Christmas,
It's just a happy slappy mishmash –
What? I've never heard of Christmas?

He goes downstage.

Look – relax about the anachronisms. We've got
permission. The playwright actually phoned up Plautus
and said, Titus Maccius, is it alright if we're not strictly
period? And Plautus answered, 'Look Pete, I wouldn't
be talking to you now if it wasn't for anachronisms.
You go ahead and use them!' So that's the way it is. If
fictional characters can't be free of historical constraints,
who can? We've got our rights.

Exit DAEMONES.

Sceparnio What's that? A mermaid? Flash of – turquoise hair;
What are you doing in my sea you beauty?
Could it be – ? Gone. Was I imagining?
Is my lust forming Venus out of seafoam?
I saw the woman in the sea! A real one!
What if it was the woman that man mourns?
And she washed breathing to my beach, strange treasure
Like floating gold I comb out of the breakers
And bring to him. Imagine his delirium;
Wouldn't he want to thank me with my freedom,
Paying my master what he paid for me,
Or slightly less, conceding wear and tear?
They'd strike a deal, speak freely with each other,
Which I can't do. The free, you get me, are
Free with the free, they understand each other;
Slaves even speak to slaves with tongues in leg-irons,

Manacled language shuffling slowly nowhere;
But if a free man asks my master for
My freedom – ! Neptune, do not drown my freedom!

Daemones (*Off.*) Slave! The roof! Slave!

*Exit SCEPARNIO. Enter LABRAX and CHARMIDES,
soaking and freezing cold. LABRAX punches CHARMIDES
and knocks him down.*

Charmides What did you do that for?

Labrax To stop you doing it to me.

Charmides I wasn't going to.

Labrax Why not?

Charmides Why should I?

Labrax If I was you I'd batter me mercilessly.

Charmides Why? Why?

Labrax Come on, think about it…

Charmides Umm…

Labrax I'm supposed to be teaching you all about
pimping, I'm your master, you're my apprentice. Now,
why did I hit you?

Charmides Um –

Labrax I'm your professor and you're my trusting student,
but then I go and get you cast up with me on this Indian
coast. Any minute now you'd have realised that! So you
see I had to hit you before you hit me.

CHARMIDES knocks LABRAX down.

What did you do that for?

Charmides Because it was my fault not yours! You were doing fine in Cyrene, it was me who begged you to take me to Barcelona to learn the tricks of the trade –

Labrax Ah, no no no, think now. Not logical.

Charmides Er…

Labrax Yes you begged me – but I needn't have listened!

Charmides Oh so it's your fault.

Labrax Correct.

Charmides So – you – should –

Labrax Yes! You've got it!

Whacks him again.

Charmides Justice has been done.

Labrax Now. You have a great deal more to learn. For example – and this is extremely important, young Charmides – the reason why I had to get out of Cyrene wasn't just to cheat Plesidippus but because I had offended – *him.*

Charmides Offended *him*? What did you do?

Labrax It was *him* I bought the girls off, but I paid *him* in fake money.

Charmides *What*? Are you mad?

Labrax Not at all. You have read your Daemones, haven't you? In *Buying Mount Olympus*, what does he say, chapter 32, page 688, just about three quarters of the way down the page.

Charmides Eh – oh – chapter 32 –

Labrax 'Do not insult the intelligence of your competitor by not taking advantage of him.'

Charmides Oh!

Labrax And what man on earth would dare to insult the
intelligence of – *him*?

Charmides What's he said about it – *him*?

Labrax To me nothing. I've never seen his face. No one
has. He doesn't need to say anything. You know what
he would do – if I hadn't drowned! See? This storm's a
blessing! Hurray for the storm! Say hurray!

Charmides Hurray.

Labrax Hurray! We have lost our boat, our girls, our
livelihood! Hurray!

Charmides What? I – don't get it –

Labrax   Listen, Charmides –
The ratio of sadness, we can say,
Is to the thing lost. Right? I lose a thimble,
I am not very sad. I lose a friend,
And I am sad according to his closeness,
His goodness, length of friendship, loyalty,
Etcetera. Maybe I am very sad,
Maybe my friend was very good to me –
But then I think, what kind of friend is he
To put me through this kind of misery?
To die and leave me grieving – is that friendly?
A better friend would take my grief away,
By never having been a friend to me.
So, for the sake of friendship, I persuade
Myself that he was not so true to me,
Not as intelligent as I remember,
Frankly a twat, not clever and not pretty.
So I take shelter from the fantasy
Of sadness in a better fantasy.
I cut the rope, he drops, and I am happy.

Charmides So if you throw me back into the sea –

Labrax No! You are not lost! You are here with me!
  Not so the trunk. Not so the girls. You see?
  Not so the boat. That is our misery.
  But do we sink again or do we build
  A better vessel from imagination
  To buoy our spirits up? The boat for starters –
  Who wants a boat that sinks? Good riddance to it!
  Shoddy contraption! What a stroke of luck
  To have got rid of that!

Charmides Oh yes I get it –

Labrax Now to the girls. Were they so beautiful?

Charmides Er –

Labrax Finished! Let's face it! Past eighteen
  A whore's a hideous has-been!
  She's like a photo that's been fingered;
  She's loitered but her looks ain't lingered.
  She may have gained experience,
  But is that what the punter wants?
  This is the mantra you must mutter:
  Innocence is our bread and butter!

Charmides Innocence is our bread and butter!

Labrax It's like cars, Charmides. You may love your old
  banger, but after a certain point it's going to cost you
  more than she's worth to keep her going. Hm? Then
  – might as well paint her blue and drive her into the sea.
  Much kinder.

Charmides Alright. But what about the trunk of money?

Labrax Money is the result of acumen. Was my acumen
  in the trunk? No. Therefore I will not be poor for long.
  It's just a matter of time.

Charmides Oh look! Another human being!

Labrax A native?

Charmides Must be! Or else a visitor!

Labrax Does he look like he eats people?

Charmides I can't tell.

Labrax Does he look friendly?

Charmides Well – er –

Labrax What's he doing?

Charmides Running towards us waving a stick and shouting. Oh! He's foaming at the mouth!

Labrax Well then so what's the answer to my question?

Charmides What was your question?

Labrax Friendly or not friendly?

Charmides Er –

Labrax I'll have to hurry you…

Charmides Not friendly!

Labrax So, get the beads out…

Charmides What beads?

Labrax Didn't you bring any beads?

Charmides He's getting nearer!

Labrax (*Patiently.*) Pebbles, then.

Charmides I don't think he wants pebbles!

Labrax (*Teacherly.*) So, what do we do?

Charmides Umm…

Labrax Come along –

Charmides Run!

Exeunt running. Enter PLESIDIPPUS.

Plesidippus Stop! Give me back my sweetheart, you
                                         dream-stealers,
Whose burnt cork boots have trampled black all over
The earth's green face, that is the unity
Of every compound heart! You have shot down
The gas balloon of the imagination.
Vermin! You have tarmacked Eden,
Screamed your cars across the garden,
Painted naked beauty's features
In a gown of tar and feathers.
Give her back! You have dissolved her
Like an aspirin, you have sold her
To the seagod, you've dispersed her
Like one drop of cochineal
In the gruel of ocean, cursed her,
And I'll crush you with my heel.
Vipers, this is how I feel!

He does a violent tapdance and staggers off.

Enter PALAESTRA, soaking wet.

Palaestra Terrific! First time I ever hang out on a beach is
when I get washed up on one.

Enter AMPELISCA the other side of the stage.

Ampelisca Got to make the best of this. Count my blessings.
On the profit side – still alive. Or is that loss?

They do not see each other and carry on soliloquising.

Palaestra Lost the one thing that told me everything. Or
could have told me. Don't cry, girl, don't blub, in terms
of salt water you're utterly upstaged here.

Ampelisca Because on the debit side, I have lost my best
friend.

Palaestra I've lost my dad! Not for the first time! First
time, I left him on a train! Poor man! Stuffed him into
the overhead compartment and when we got to the
station, leapt off without him! Sorry mate! Luckily he
turned up in lost property. The parental section.

Ampelisca Why didn't she swim? Was she thinking
about something else? The casket with her dad in it! Or
maybe she couldn't even swim! I haven't got the faintest
idea! She's my best friend and I don't even know if
she can swim. No, not my best friend, my only friend.
There is a difference.

Palaestra Take some advice from old Palaestra, get
yourself a father who floats! And who isn't made out
of bits of stuff. And don't shove him into a box and get
yourself shipwrecked. Have you got all that? Poor old
fool. I've kept him with me all over the world since I
was three, now he's gone forever! And my best friend's
bobbing about in there. Not my best friend, my only
friend. Oh where are you Ampelisca?

Ampelisca Going back in. What's the point? No – I won't
be able to drown. I'm a good swimmer, not like her, the
brilliant sinker, the Olympic drowner.

Palaestra I have even lost my pimp, how on earth am I
going to live? Do they have tarts like me in this country,
or only to eat at teatime? Cannibals. That's how it'll
be. Don't know how far we was washed. This could be
anywhere, this could be – England! In which case we're
finished. They'll have us with chips. They'll batter us.

Ampelisca But then, what kind of life have I had? Sweet
sixteen and never been kissed. Everything else to
excess.

Palaestra Suicide. Easy once you've decided. Just the
other side of the coin. All the effort you put into staying

25

alive you switch over, stop kicking back and join in with the kickers.

Ampelisca Terrible to throw away someone else's property but I see no future for this particular body.

Palaestra No more domination. No more rubber love. What a relief! Goodbye!

Ampelisca Goodbye!

Palaestra That's a good echo. Goodbye!

Ampelisca Goodbye!

Palaestra I suppose that is an echo –

Ampelisca I suppose that is an echo –

Palaestra Are you an echo, or –

Ampelisca Are you an echo, or –

Palaestra Thought so!

Ampelisca Thought so!

Palaestra Just checking!

Ampelisca Just checking!

Palaestra (*Aside.*) I'll try and catch it out.

Ampelisca (*Aside.*) I'll try and catch it out.

Palaestra The tirpitz is a thin-skinned vessel!

Ampelisca The tirpitz is a thin-skinned vessel!

Palaestra No it isn't!

Ampelisca Yes it is!

Palaestra Aha!

Ampelisca Palaestra!

Palaestra Ampelisca, is that you? It's me, Palaestra.

Ampelisca What! Where are you?

Palaestra I don't know!

Ampelisca Nor do I! Try to find your way over to me!

Palaestra I'm trying!

Ampelisca Isn't it brilliant in plays when the actors let you know it's night by pretending they can't see each other?

Palaestra Yes, I love it when they do that. Where are you, where are you, Ampelisca? But it's not night.

Ampelisca No of course it's not for the audience, but it is for us, in the play.

Palaestra No it's not night in the play, you soft witch, it's still morning.

Ampelisca Oh there you are Palaestra!

Palaestra Ampelisca!

They rush into each others arms.

Ampelisca I thought you'd drowned!

Palaestra I thought you'd drowned!

Ampelisca I thought you were an echo!

Palaestra I thought you were an echo!

Ampelisca We've got to snap out of this.

Palaestra Yes we have.

Ampelisca There, done it.

Palaestra Done it.

Ampelisca Palaestra!

Palaestra Ampelisca! My life passed before my eyes.

Ampelisca What was it like?

Palaestra Disgusting. I thought, I'm too young to be watching this.

Ampelisca We've lost everything.

Palaestra Don't be soft. We lost that long ago. In it's place we got nothing and rubbish. And that's what we've now lost.

Ampelisca We've lost the man. We've lost Labrax.

Palaestra Oh no! Haha! I wish I'd seen him, spluttering, thrashing his arms. Help me, help me! Shark swims off with his legs – I say, come back with my Italian shoes! Another one bites off his hands – come back with my cigarette holder!

Ampelisca You've lost your dad!

Palaestra So? At the end of the day, dear, he was a scrap of tarpaulin in a wooden box.

Ampelisca What about your vow?

Palaestra What vow?

Ampelisca You vowed you'd never marry till you find your father.

Palaestra Well yeah there is that.

Ampelisca So now you'll have to be a tart forever.

Palaestra S'pose so.

Ampelisca Don't you care about anything?

Palaestra No.

Ampelisca That's coz you're not freeborn.

Palaestra I am freeborn.

Ampelisca Well yes but you were sold at the age of three and anyway now you've lost the proof.

Palaestra I was stolen, not sold!

Ampelisca So you reckon.

Palaestra That's what they told me!

Ampelisca Who? The pimps who gave you your name? Palaestra. It means 'exercise yard'.

Palaestra Shut up!

Ampelisca Sorry love, I just thought nothing mattered to you. Not even the fact that you've lost the box that tells you who your father is.

Palaestra I will know him when I see him.

Ampelisca But will he know you?

Palaestra I remember him.

Ampelisca You were three!

Palaestra I remember him!

Ampelisca What was he like?

Palaestra Well you know Zeus?

Ampelisca Yes…

Palaestra He wasn't like that.

Ampelisca Oh.

Palaestra More like Apollo. In fact exactly like Apollo.

Ampelisca Oh God!

Palaestra Yes.

Ampelisca Well that would explain one thing.

PETER OSWALD

Palaestra What?

Ampelisca Why you didn't care about losing the young
man in Cyrene who wanted to buy you. Well he wasn't
even immortal!

Palaestra He comes up to me in the street, says, I am in
love with you. I'm like – and?

Ampelisca I'm like – what?

Palaestra I'm like *so* 'and?'

Ampelisca I'm like *so* 'what?'

Palaestra Whatever.

Palaestra Now there's no future for us, love, and judging
by the past, that's good news. You think I don't care?
I do care. I don't want the last thing I see to be some
savage covering you with mustard. Our life's been
horrible, but it can get worse. We are good friends.
That's all life's given us. Take my hand now and let's
walk back into the wet.

Ampelisca Yes. Oh. What's that?

Palaestra A shrine to – oh, Venus.

Ampelisca Goodbye Venus.

Palaestra Bitch.

Ampelisca No!

Palaestra Cow.

Ampelisca No!

Palaestra Look what she did to us!

Ampelisca Don't speak like that about the goddess! If we
ask her nicely she still might save us! Save us, Venus!
Please.

No response. They go towards the sea. Enter
PTOLEMOCRATIA.

Ptolemocratia Oh Venus you have spoken in a dream
– Look out!

Ampelisca What?

Ptolemocratia The cliff is very weak there! Move away
from it! Phew! One day that will be the death of
somebody, and I expect it will be a fate richly deserved!
But it is not your fate yet.
Who are you people?

Ampelisca We shall not deceive
A priestess. We are prostitutes, transported
Out of Cyrene for the Spanish market.

Ptolemocratia Neptune condemned your craft.

Ampelisca We think our owner
Is lost at sea. But Zeus has judged us worthy
Of merely being wet.

Ptolemocratia I praise his justice.
What do you plan to do?

Ampelisca With us, priestess,
Is it not so much what we want that matters,
As what is wished for us.

PTOLEMOCRATIA goes into a trance.

Goddess from the sea of grace,
Lonely islands made your face,
And the womblight of the deep
Made your eyes where drowned men sleep.
Look at what your tide has brought us!
What are your wishes for these daughters?

Palaestra What does she say?

31

Ampelisca　　　　　　What does she say?

Ptolemocratia　　　　　　　　She wishes
You warm and well.

Ampelisca　　　　Then she will have my service!

*Exeunt into the shrine. Enter LABRAX and CHARMIDES,
running.*

Labrax　What does he want?

Charmides　He wants to kill us!

Labrax　He doesn't even know us!

Charmides　Maybe the news has spread!

Labrax　What news?

Charmides　The news about us!

Labrax　And what sort of news is that?

Charmides　The news that we deserve to be killed!

Labrax　That's just a rumour.

Charmides　Maybe it's *him*!

Labrax　*Him*? *Him*? You don't understand *him*. *He* would
not chase us down a beach! Perhaps it is someone who
has been sent by *him* –

Enter PLESIDIPPUS.

Charmides　Oh! It's Plesidippus!

Labrax　So we are not lost! This is our own coast!

Plesidippus　Minotaurs! You must give me back my bride
Or I will tear your eyes out of your skulls!

Labrax　(*Aside.*) Charmides, pick up a rock and hide it
behind your back.

Plesidippus Give me my sweetheart! Let me touch her flesh,
If it is colder than these rocks, these rocks
Are at least solid, are not abstract frost;
Nothing is colder than the abstract – ice
Freezes your breath, but the unrealised,
Unreachable unfleshed abstract of ice
Makes your whole spirit an eternal arctic!

Labrax (*Aside.*) He's gone raving mad, Charmides. I'll do
the best I can.

Plesidippus Where have you put her beauty? Faith is staggered
That Neptune in his furnace of green fire
Preserved you true born corpses and burned her!

Labrax Plesidippus, if she is dead – and our being alive
might tempt you to hope otherwise if bereavement was
not such a glorious delirium – if she is dead, well then
so is the relationship, let's start thinking about how to
get you another wife.

Plesidippus Another? You have taken all my money –
Almost! That is my secondary sadness,
Which, wedded with the first, adds up to madness!

Labrax Look, she was Bakewell, mate, she was total tart, all
jam and pastry, she's done it with lobsters!

Plesidippus Why me? Why me?

Labrax Because we saw you coming a mile away! Forgive
us, Plesidippus! How could we resist it! A man who falls
in love with a prostitute!

Plesidippus Aaaagghhhh!

Labrax Run for it!

> *Exeunt LABRAX and CHARMIDES, running.
> CHARMIDES throws a rock, that hits PLESIDIPPUS on
> the head. He staggers off the way he came, clutching his head
> and crying out.*

Enter SCEPARNIO.

Sceparnio The free man wakes. He wakes early, he
wakes late. He wakes when he likes. He springs down
the corridor. Is the bathroom free? It is! At breakfast,
a letter from a beautiful woman. Are you free this
afternoon? I am free anytime, day or night, I am a free
man! He goes down to the supermarket in search of free
offers. Only joking! The free man is a man of means.
He has a disposable income, and plenty of free time.
What shall he do? He will go swimming. He will swim
freestyle. He pops into the church for a prayer. The Free
Church. His coat snags on a nail but he easily flicks it
free because he is a free man, from the free world, as it
used to be called, in the past of your present, which is
my future, if I have one.

Cos I'm not free,
No my time is not my own,
I live in slavery,
I ain't got a free bone
In my body.

Neptune, sweet sea,
Don't you keep that free man's bride,
You got the lovely
Sand to kiss with your tide,
You don't need she.

*Enter AMPELISCA in sacred robes from the shrine with
a jar.*

What? That is not the priestess. Christ! It must be Venus
herself.

He crosses himself.

I have never seen anything – I have never *seen* anything
until this moment, it was just kind of hearing vague
rumours of things through my eyes – God now every

hair on my head is an eye, every inch of my skin is retina.

He sees AMPELISCA going near the weak place on the cliff.

Sceparnio Woah! This way, this way – little bit more – yup, yup – phew!

Ampelisca I forgot! The crumbling cliff edge!

Sceparnio Hello.

Ampelisca Hello.

Sceparnio You are a virgin.

Ampelisca Er –

Sceparnio One of the virgins of Venus. What's your name?

Ampelisca Constance. What's yours?

Sceparnio Sceparnio.

Ampelisca That's nice.

Sceparnio Well I'm going to change it when I –

Ampelisca When you what?

Sceparnio Think of something more appropriate.

Ampelisca Do you live here?

Sceparnio Yes. I am privileged and contented to make my abode in this house.

Ampelisca What, the one with no roof?

Sceparnio Oh there is a roof! A beautiful roof! There it is – over in Italy.

Ampelisca Then there isn't a roof.

Sceparnio Really? Not? I mean what if – heaven forbid – your dress blew off –

Ampelisca Heaven forbid!

Sceparnio You would not say you did not have a dress.

Ampelisca That would depend on how far away it blew, wouldn't it? If it blew right into the sea –

Sceparnio Heaven forbid!

Ampelisca Revealing my pristine nakedness, and sank, that would be it. It if just flopped round my feet –

Sceparnio Heaven forbid!

Ampelisca Nestling against my delicate ankles, then it wouldn't be totally lost. Unless I then kicked it lightly over the hedge, exposing the sleek firmness of my inner thighs, and a panther tore it to pieces.

Sceparnio That would be sad!

Ampelisca Or if I bent over and it ripped right up the back, so that the perfection of my slim waist and lovely shoulders was all too apparent –

Sceparnio That would be tragic.

Ampelisca Or if it simply tore itself off me and wandered off into the forest crying, Where am I, where am I? Then it would be lost.

Sceparnio But still yours.

Ampelisca Mine. But not mine. Like my life.

Sceparnio Oh?

Ampelisca Could I have some water?

Sceparnio No.

Ampelisca Oh.

Sceparnio I mean you can't have any – yet.

Ampelisca What does a person have to do?

Sceparnio Chat!

Ampelisca Oh I see. You don't get many passers-by here.

Sceparnio We are lucky to live in the country! We have a real community, us and the priestess, though she only pokes her head out once every six months.

Ampelisca And are you free?

Sceparnio Sure! Are you?

Ampelisca No.

Sceparnio Oh.

Ampelisca I serve Venus.

Sceparnio I think this is just the most incredible coincidence!

Ampelisca What is?

Sceparnio That you should happen to walk by here and just at that moment, so do I!

Ampelisca In what way is that a coincidence?

Sceparnio I mean that you, looking and speaking exactly as you do, should bump into me, looking and speaking exactly as I do. Strange, eh?

Ampelisca In what way?

Sceparnio I mean I do think it's extraordinary that we should have met. I a free man and you a – when did you get here?

Ampelisca Last night.

Sceparnio Oh! Oh no, what if it's – ! Have you been shipwrecked? Has a free man bought your freedom so

he can marry you? Is his name Platypus – recidivist
– Plesidippus?

Ampelisca No! Are you mad?

Sceparnio Oh God!

Ampelisca That's my mate.

Sceparnio Your mate? Your mate? Where is she? Drowned?

Ampelisca No she's in there crying.

Sceparnio Liberty! Oh God, please don't tell him!

Ampelisca Who?

Sceparnio Polygamous! Pleasure Palace! Let me tell him!
It's my plan!

Ampelisca For what reason?

Sceparnio To get my freedom!

Ampelisca Oh, so you're not free.

Sceparnio No. Sorry. Oh! I thought you meant, are you
free at the moment, for a moment, kind of thing – um –

Ampelisca Freeborn?

Sceparnio No.

Ampelisca Scum.

Sceparnio I will get you water if you promise to let me tell
him! Oh so much water! Why is she crying?

Ampelisca She has something in a trunk which proves
who her father is if she can ever find him. It's gone
down. No proof now. And she was too young to
remember. Freeborn but can't prove it.

Sceparnio That's a good reason to cry!

Ampelisca Free eh? I never believed it! What's your master like?

Sceparnio Poor. Depressed. Yours?

Ampelisca Drowned. I hope. Pimp.

Sceparnio Pimp.

Ampelisca Yeah! Look, I'm not your new neighbour, sorry about that. And my name's not Constance, in fact the reality of me is about as far from this appearance as you could possibly get.

Sceparnio I never want to be any distance from your appearance ever again for the rest of my life. Look, are we friends? I can't tell! I really like you.

Ampelisca I'd have loved you if you were free.

Sceparnio But you are not free yourself.

Ampelisca Freeborn. Look, get me the water.

Sceparnio Damn! Damn! Then how much money would it cost for me to have sex with you?

Ampelisca Straight shag fifteen quid. With top off, twenty-five quid.

Sceparnio Kiss?

Ampelisca Unhygienic.

Exit SCEPARNIO with jug.

Or am I free? It seemed much easier
To say I am a slave, but am I really?
Who owns me now? The sea has drowned my owner,
So the sea owns me. But the sea can't see;
To be a blind man's slave is to be free.
So I must come to a decision then,
Freely – about – my heart is hunting me

Like a dog sniffing for a dead thing. Hurry
And find me heart, so that love can devour me.
No! Not so fast! Help! Slavery
Come back! A possibility
Explosing is engulfing me,
Freedom and democracy,
Enterprise, romance, dignity,
A house, a husband; two or three;
Security, mobility;
What if I make the wrong decision?
What if I choose the wrong religion
And end up in the wrong heaven?
Oh my sweet goddess what's that running along the beach?

Enter PTOLEMOCRATIA.

Ptolemocratia Oh Venus you have spoken in a dream…

Ampelisca It's the pimps! Someone's chasing them! Save
me Venus!

Ptolemocratia Into the shrine quickly.

Exit into shrine.

Monsters desire my once and future maidens.
It shall not be! The belly of the dragon
Shall not be beautified by these once chained
Then freed by Venus through the ocean's passion!
And Venus, you have spoken in a dream
To me, and after all this time it seems
I am to find true love. Who it will be
I do not know, but I have been awarded
In recognition of my understanding,
Slowly engrossed in patience and in pain,
True love: and I will know him by his crying.

*Enter DAEMONES dragging SCEPARNIO who is carrying
the full jug.*

Daemones Still no damn roof!

DAEMONES is embarrassed to see PTOLEMOCRATIA.

Oh!

SCEPARNIO takes his chance to slip into the shrine.

Can I believe my eyes? Priestess! Many a day since last your eyes saw the light of day! I have been reduced to imaginary conversations. Or have you been away?

Ptolemocratia Good morning Mr Daemones. I have, in a sense, been away, in consultation with my goddess.

Daemones In a trance?

Ptolemocratia Call it that.

Daemones (*Aside.*) Fantastic. One neighbour and she's generally transcendent. But I do like her. She's a mystery I want to get to the bottom of. So what has drawn you out?

Ptolemocratia Love.

Daemones For whom?

Ptolemocratia Love that inspires the wren fight the eagle.

Daemones Oh you've come out to do some birdwatching. I have stored up so many questions to ask you, priestess.

Ptolemocratia Please ask, Mr Daemones.

Daemones Venus! Ha! Venus! Why Venus?

Ptolemocratia Why here?

Daemones I would have thought she was more of an urban goddess, divinity of backstreets and boudoirs.

Ptolemocratia She was born out of the seafoam.

Daemones Right! I had never considered that aspect of her! Even Venus was a virgin once! Haha! So this is the shrine of Venus Virgin. I had never considered virginity to form any part of the venereal religion.

Ptolemocratia We worship her in all her forms.

Daemones Exciting! But this brings me to my next question. Perhaps a delicate one? May I?

Ptolemocratia I am open.

Daemones You do not appear to be married. I never see any comings and goings. Now to be perfectly frank – can celibacy really form any part of the full blooded worship of Venus?

Ptolemocratia Who says I am celibate?

Daemones Ah!

Ptolemocratia It is just that the goddess has not yet chosen for me the man I am to love.

Daemones (*Aside.*) Better hurry up!

Ptolemocratia May I ask you, Mr Daemones, what has made you suddenly so curious about Venus? We have been neighbours for some years.

Daemones I had a dream last night.

Ptolemocratia Go on.

Daemones I dreamed that your shrine was blown by the wind right up against my house, and we could see through our windows into your windows. Strange.

Ptolemocratia A prophecy of this conversation.

Daemones Possibly, possibly. It made me think how little I know about Venus! I mean I've never never peeped into your windows, never mind stepped into your shrine! Venus. Venus.

Ptolemocratia Were you never married, Mr Daemones?

Daemones Ha!

He fights back tears.

Ptolemocratia Are you crying?

Daemones Me? No! Married. Yes. It was not so much a marriage of convenience as a convenience marriage, attractively packaged and swiftly consumed. But! But! There was a novelty gift included, and that I did keep – for a while – till it was stolen –

Ptolemocratia You mean a child?

Daemones No tears. Look. All gone. Too much brine around here anyway.

Ptolemocratia I have acquired two children overnight, out of the sea, but I can't look after them, everything I have I am given by the goddess. Offerings of food or oil from time to time. They are terribly hungry.

Daemones You'll have to talk to the slave. I don't get involved. Children?

Ptolemocratia Daughters.

Daemones How old are they?

Ptolemocratia They are both twenty-two.

Daemones Ugly?

Ptolemocratia Not at all.

Daemones Perhaps I'll bring some bread round. As an offering.

Ptolemocratia To Venus?

Daemones It is alright? Can people do that?

Ptolemocratia Of course Mr Daemones! I didn't know you were a believer! If you like, at our next festival you can carry the candles.

Daemones Candles? I was imgining something to do with seafoam and me dressing up as Mars.

Ptolemocratia I am not sure you have grasped the principles of our religion, Mr Daemones. I told you very clearly that this is the shrine of Venus Virgin.

Daemones Oh come on, I mean she was a virgin once, fine, for about five minutes. Don't tell me it's not all –

Ptolemocratia All what?

Daemones Sceparnio! Damn! Where are you!

Enter SCEPARNIO propelled out of the temple by PALAESTRA.

Palaestra No slaves in the temple!

Ptolemocratia Just what I need!

She takes the jug off him and enters into the shrine.

Sceparnio Sir, sir – Plesidippus! Where? Where?

Daemones Plesidippus?

Sceparnio Sir, sir!

Daemones What?

Sceparnio Sell me my freedom!

Daemones Not now!

Sceparnio Please!

Daemones I do not think you are ready for it. Freedom is complicated.

Sceparnio I will prove myself worthy!

Daemones How?

Sceparnio Sir – if I was to restore to a certain gentleman, a free gentleman, like yourself, a lady most dear to him – would you consider me worthy of admission to the league of the free?

Daemones It might impress me, I don't know. I don't know myself, Sceparnio. You know I am adrift, becalmed, a mesmerised helmsman circumnavigating nothing! You know why, you know I have no answers to the incessant questions that blankness and darkness insist on asking, you know that I lost my – you know what I have lost through my own miscalculation, that I am therefore forbidden to intervene in the troubles of the world, and yet you, who have not even fixed my roof, come battering with notions of freedom! I have two hawsers still, this house and yourself. One of them is roofless and the other one cries to me to cut through and cast it away! Do you think it would be easy for me not to own anyone? I cannot do it, Sceparnio.

Sceparnio I'm sorry about the roof, sir! It's just that things have been happening!

Daemones What kind of things?

Sceparnio A woman – asked me for water!

Daemones Is that so devastating?

Sceparnio Sir, I have got the water out of the well no problem, but I can't get her out of my mind!

Daemones How long ago was this?

Sceparnio A few minutes ago.

Daemones And you predict that you will still be thinking about her a few minutes from now?

Sceparnio I love her sir!

Daemones And what does she think of you?

Sceparnio She says she would love me if I was free!

Daemones Ah. So it is she that wants you to be free, not you. I wish you had told me that in the first place. Sceparnio, you are young, you have not seen many women. In Cyrene this one would probably not be very good looking.

Sceparnio No! Oh well, you've convinced me, sir!

Daemones Have I?

Sceparnio Yes! Why throw away the only thing I own, my slavery, for the sake of someone who only wants me if I'm free! What a tart! Honestly!

Daemones Good boy!

Sceparnio And she's got our jug.

Daemones Well go and get it back.

Sceparnio Into the temple? A slave? No sir, please!

Daemones No arguing. Go and get it!

Sceparnio Must I?

Exeunt, SCEPARNIO into the shrine and DAEMONES into his house. Enter PALAESTRA and AMPELISCA from the shrine, peeping over the cliff, terrified.

Palaestra Where are they? Where?

Ampelisca Mind the weak place!

Palaestra I can't see them!

Ampelisca Maybe they were running back to Cyrene.

Palaestra Goodbye.

Ampelisca Now we can stay here and be priestesses of
Venus!

Palaestra Wonderful.

Ampelisca And I'll marry Sceparnio.

Palaestra What – the slave?

Ampelisca What does that matter?

Palaestra It doesn't matter at all! I mean it wouldn't matter if
he wasn't a lying git. But to be a slave and a lying git –

Ampelisca He seems like a git because he's a slave.

Palaestra I mean come on, he told you he was a free man so
he could have his way with you!

Ampelisca Yeah. Disgraceful.

Palaestra Insist he gets his freedom first. Then if he's still a
git you know that wasn't the reason.

Ampelisca I won't let him near me till he is what he said he
was.

Palaestra Good girl.

Ampelisca What about you and Plesidippus?

Palaestra Well what about it? Have I found my dad?

Palaestra Watch the cliff-edge.

Ampelisca Aaaagghhhh!

Palaestra What?

Ampelisca They're coming back!

Exeunt. Enter LABRAX and CHARMIDES.

Labrax You're sure he was dead?

Charmides Totally. I went back and checked didn't I?

Labrax There. Good. All is well.

Charmides Except for *him.*

Labrax *Him*? No, he thinks I've drowned! Hahaha! Silly old *him*!

Charmides Some say *he* doesn't even exist.

Labrax Many people have proved *his* existence by the cessation of their own. Let us not take *his* name is vain, let us not chortle at the mention of *him*.

Charmides You just did.

Labrax Well then I deserve a lingering and upleasant death.

Charmides I don't think *he* heard you! And I won't tell *him*!

Labrax Haha. You'd better not. Hoho.

Enter SCEPARNIO from temple.

Sceparnio Calls herself a priestess of Venus, but when a young man in love steps into her shrine she turns totally Vestal – no you can't have your jug back, na na na, that wasn't the reason you came in here, clear off and don't come back unless asked. What! Of course I didn't go in there to get the jug back. But I want the jug back. I don't know what's the matter with them.

Labrax With whom?

Sceparnio With those girls clinging to the altar of Venus and sobbing, don't give us back to those horrible men!

Labrax It's them!

He surreptitiously takes out his gun and goes into the shrine.

Sceparnio Oh. That must have been one of the horrible men.

Charmides No, I wouldn't say so! He is direct, always, in his manner, he knows his mind, certainly. But horrible? No, no, no –

Sceparnio Well what does he want? What do you want?

Charmides Oh I'm glad you asked me that! Please, please! A place to sleep!

Sceparnio Sleep anywhere you like.

Charmides Look, it's freezing! I'm soaked!

Sound of screaming from the shrine.

Sceparnio (*Aside.*) What do I do? I've got to let Plesidippus know she's here, but where is he? (*To CHARMIDES.*) What?

Charmides I said look I'm soaked. Take me in, can't you, into the house, give me some dry clothes.

Sceparnio Look you can have this mat.

Renewed screaming. SCEPARNIO shouts.

Plesidippus! Plesidippus!

Charmides What?

Sceparnio I said you can have this mat. You can wear it while you dry your clothes off.

Charmides What? (*Screaming from inside shrine.*) I'm not giving you my clothes!

Sceparnio Then give me back my mat! I'm not letting you have my very own mat for nothing!

Charmides You're a pervert you are!

Sceparnio Don't try to make me feel bad!

Screaming.

Charmides What?

Sceparnio I said don't try to make me feel bad. I know
what you want to do.

Charmides What?

Sceparnio Leave me alone! Plesidippus! Plesidippus!

Charmides Now what's going on in this shrine?

Exit to shrine.

Sceparnio My sweetheart screaming in the shrine!
But the priestess has forbidden me to go in there!
Plesidippus could! You can't keep a free man out!
(*Calls.*) Plesidippus! Plesidippus! He's either dead or out
of earshot, in which case there's no way on earth I can
reach him! Never has been! If a person's out of range of
the sound of your voice, you can't speak to him, that's
that, you can project and enunciate until your brain
bursts, you're basically talking to yourself! Oh if only
a hand would reach out of the future with some as yet
undreamed-of device by means of which you can speak
to a person who isn't there! Will such a miracle ever
exist? Then I could save my sweetheart!

Audience member hands him a mobile phone.

What? Cordless? That's amazing! How does it – er –

Audience member explains phone.

Great! So – what's his number? Oh well that's useless!
I'll have to go and look for him myself, using my
classical eyes and my ancient Greek feet! At the end of
the day you can only rely on yourself.

Exit.

*Doors of the shrine open. LABRAX has the jug over his
head and his hands tied in front. PTOLEMOCRATIA has*

the gun on CHARMIDES whose hands are tied behind.
PALAESTRA and AMPELISCA enter behind.

Ptolemocratia Venus! Accept this living sacrifice
Of wickedness. I shall not stain your altars
With their unholy blood, but I will force them,
Awed by your power, to forswear their calling!

LABRAX bellows something.

What was that? A confession? What did he say?

Charmides (*Embarrassed.*) Er, he said, Madam if you don't
mind I am supposed to be at a synchronised swimming
lesson.

Ptolemocratia Fiends, you shall not swim out of my coercion
Till you have synchronised an oath to Venus,
Mother of true love, not to trade in women
Ever again! Not to tear down the veil
Of heaven which *is* heaven since in heaven
The surface is the centre – so the skin
Of woman is her spirit and division
Of soul and body is not possible!
She is suffused with beauty like a towel
Left in the dew beside a swimming pool.
It is in spirit that you trade, my fiend,
And not in flesh, since there is no such thing!

Charmides There is if I'm poking it. Sorry.

Ptolemocratia Flesh, if *you* clutch it, is as spiritless
As flesh can be, since lust drives out the spirit!

Charmides Mine's a screwdriver!

Ptolemocratia You have debased these children of the goddess,
Beg for forgiveness!

Charmides   But – We rescued them!
We found them working in Cyrene, lady,
That famous naval base, that noble city,

Which every payday is awash with seamen.
And we were taking them to Barcelona, where no one
baths alone! Sorry. No I mean that place is heaving with
wealthy matadors, with enormous swords, strumming
guitars; after a year a tart can buy herself out and go
independent. That's like marriage that is but with her
own chequebook. Sorry. Isn't that right though, Labrax?

LABRAX mumbles and shakes his head.

He's my boss, I'm straight out of pimp school, I don't
know anything about it. What was it you wanted us to
swear again?

Ptolemocratia Nothing! Till you have seen the cloudless
brightness
Of Venus, like a star stripped of all distance.

Charmides What? We're going to see Venus? With her kit
off? Sorry.

Ptolemocratia Mother, restorer of virginity
To whores who fall worn-out into the sea
From which you rose – appear to us we pray,
To strike your grace into these stoneblind thieves,
Teach them truth by means of terror!

Charmides We'll never be the same again, Labrax!

Ptolemocratia What are you saying, goddess, by this silence?

Charmides Nothing?

Ptolemocratia Nothing!

LABRAX roars something.

What? What?

Charmides Er, he said, That's always been my complaint
about religion. At the end of the day it can't match up to a
good handjob.

At this point two demi-goddesses appear, carrying a dead pigeon.

Oh! Labrax! Labrax! Something's happening!

The demi-godesses dance around.

There's these two birds, Labrax! No, three birds, but one of them's dead. I mean – there's these two semi-divine beings, Labrax! What? How do I know they're semi-divine? Well I don't, they could be entirely divine! But they're semi-clad. Ok, two totally divine, semi-clad beings are dancing around – it's amazing – yes I'll ask them if they're looking for work.

The demi-godesses lay the pigeon on the altar.

They're playing catch the pigeon. What? Didn't I mention the pigeon?

They leave.

They've gone. No, they've left the pigeon behind. No, it's not cooing, it's dead. Well I'm sorry about that!

Ptolemocratia Venus attempting to descend, one dove
Of the ten million in her team, was stricken
By your proximity and died. The goddess,
Fearing the death of all the rest, like songbirds
In a coal mine, withdrew. We shall not see her
Again while you afflict earth's atmosphere!

PTOLEMOCRATIA in despair sinks to her knees, letting the gun fall to the floor. CHARMIDES kicks the gun from her and dribbles it over to LABRAX who picks it up.

Fiends! I was praying!

Charmides Sorry.

CHARMIDES guides LABRAX as to where to point the gun.

53

Right – right – that's it, you've got it, right on the tit.
Come on girls, shuffle off with us or the religious leader
gets it.

Ampelisca Priestess!

Ptolemocratia Venus! Venus!

Enter DAEMONES, not noticing the gun.

Daemones I have just had the most amazing daydream.
As I was lying on my bedroom floor,
Crossing the gulf to lunch by magic carpet,
Suddenly I was looking at a monkey
Monkeying up a drainpipe. It was planning
To thrust its fist into a swallow's nest,
But it could not quite reach it, so it said,
'Excuse me mister, could I use your ladder?'
'Certainly not,' I cried, 'I am from Athens,
And swallows are from Athens, they are Procne
And Philomela's children.' Then the monkey
Chattered and blustered at me, threatening
To have me bang to rights, and so I grabbed her
Around the waist, and got a chain around her,
And dragged her off! The dream's interpretation
Is not, I think, explicit.

Ptolemocratia   Yes it is!
This is the meaning of your dream: you must
Get back into your house as quick as swanflight!

Daemones Eh? All right. Hey, you with the jug, be careful
if you're strolling by the cliff, there's a weak place. (*Aside.*)
There's a weak place in every plot, but in this case, the
weak place *is* the plot. I mean the weak place in the cliff is
an important part of the plot – um –

Exit.

Ptolemocratia Girls, run! Let him shoot me!

Charmides Right a bit, Labrax. Now point – the gun – at your own head – and pull – the trigger –

LABRAX makes a kind of lowing sound.

Do – it – Labrax – it's – our – only – chance –

LABRAX makes more bellowing noises.

Point – the gun – down your trousers –

LABRAX bellows and shakes his head.

Alright – put – the – gun – on – the – floor. Just – do it – trust me.

LABRAX puts the gun down. PLESIDIPPUS steps forward from behind CHARMIDES and picks it up.

Plesidippus Ha! It was me behind him all the time, Instructing him to utter my instructions!

Charmides He shoved a gun into my back!

Plesidippus   What gun?

LABRAX says something.

Charmides I know I said that. I didn't know what advances in medicine were about to happen!

Enter DAEMONES.

Daemones That's odd. I could swear the man with the jug on his head had a gun in his hand.

Plesidippus He did! I took it off him!

Daemones Strange things happen in the temple of Venus. Is it real or a vision?

He takes it off PLESIDIPPUS.

Seems real enough, but no doubt it will turn into a finch and fly off the second I step out of this place.

Exit. PLESIDIPPUS sees PALAESTRA.

Plesidippus Who is this one whose eyes I recognise,
Who seems alive, though she whose face this is,
Died in the night, and in my churchyard heart
On an invisible lychgate lay stretched out.
Was it the force of my desire that raised her
Out of the deep? This proves my true love's power!
Ha? My love!

*CHARMIDES has cut loose his hands with a knife.
LABRAX tries to take off the jug but it's stuck.*

Charmides Right girls – Barcelona!

Re-enter DAEMONES, without the gun.

Daemones Where the hell is Sceparnio? What on earth's
going on?

Plesidippus Mr Daemones, have you got the gun?

Daemones No.

Plesidippus Would you get it please, immediately!

Daemones No I will not. I have no truck with guns,
They are decisive instruments of change;
I never get involved with anything.

Charmides Who is this man?

Daemones   Daemones is my name.

Charmides Not *the* Daemones? Oh I am extremely
Pleased, sir! So this is where you have been hiding?
Financial genius! Gave away his fortune!

Daemones Commerce! My head hurts!

Charmides To quote your great work, *Buying Mount
Olympus*, Slavery is central to the free market economy.
What else do you say – er – The poor are poor because

they *want* to be poor. Love is the only commodity that retains its scarcity value despite being ubiquitous. That was a real wake-up call to me that was! Inspired me to be a pimp! Thank you! Thank you! Thank you! Sorry.

The pimps are about to exit.

Enter SCEPARNIO.

Sceparnio Stop! The whole place is surrounded by policemen! I couldn't find Plesidippus – oh there he is – but then I suddenly realised, a crime has been committed!

Charmides What crime?

Sceparnio Ampelisca is freeborn!

Palaestra So am I!

Charmides Can you prove it?

Palaestra Well –

Charmides Ha!

Plesidippus Where were you born?

Palaestra / Ampelisca Athens!

Plesidippus Then, love, you are both Roman citizens,
And to enslave you is a capital crime!

Charmides You say the place is surrounded by coppers?

Sceparnio Yes, and they would come bursting in, if we had enough actors!

Daemones Is there a spare actor here?

Is there a policeman?

(*If not:*) Ok pickpockets, that's your cue! (*Etc.*)

VOLUNTEER found and taken backstage. Company goes back a few lines. Re-enter VOLUNTEER, with aeroplane wings strapped to his shoulders.

Charmides You don't look like a policeman!

Volunteer I'm in plane clothes.

Daemones We are terribly sorry. That joke was actually extremely funny in ancient Greece.

Sceparnio Take them away!

Charmides Oh well, Labrax! Another interview with the most bored people on earth.

Plesidippus Move!

Charmides See you again soon!

Plesidippus No you will not! Palaestra, right this moment
Scour his atrocious face out of your mind,
This is the first instruction of your husband,
Lovingly, tenderly but firmly given,
So that we two can make a fresh beginning!
I love you more than the earth loves the sun!
If you love me, you must blot out this person!

Palaestra Oh. Er, right.

Plesidippus Now I must go with the police to give
Evidence. But I will return like lightning!

Exeunt.

Sceparnio Sir, forgive me but I don't feel it's right for these two girls who've just been rescued from the ocean to be sheltering in that freezing shrine with the Priestess. Couldn't they stay with us?

Ptolemocratia They are not going anywhere!

Ampelisca Oh please, priestess!

Sceparnio The roof's off but we've got a downstairs and a lovely fire and chocolate hobnobs.

Palaestra We won't be far away.

Sceparnio Sir?

Daemones I am indifferent.

Ampelisca I am Ampelisca, sir.

Palaestra I am Palaestra.

Daemones Palaestra! Exercise yard! (*Aside.*) I suppose the nearest equivalent in English would be Jim.

Exeunt PALAESTRA and DAEMONES into his house. Exit priestess into shrine.

Sceparnio Ampelisca – you are free!

Ampelisca Sceparnio, you are not!

Exeunt into house. Enter Weather Girls.

Sun There will now be a short

Rain Break in the weather.

Sun During this brief lull

Rain The tea and coffee will be hot

Sun But cold ice cream patches

Rain And showers of chocolate nuts

Sun Can be expected.

Rain Please enjoy the calm weather.

Sun The Storm will resume in fifteen minutes.

Second Part

Enter the WEATHER.

Weather The weather at the end of time
Will be ferociously sublime,
As the last sunset gently spreads
Its greens its yellows and its reds
And the last sky, tomb of all skies,
Like a bright parrot droops and dies
As the sun, roaring, ragged, grand,
Touches the scorched horizon and
The entire globe goes up in flames,
With all its blessings and its blames,
A blazing ball of fire that turns
In a great smoke ring as it burns,
Till there is nothing but a drifting
Of ashes through the star-sieve sifting,
As if the world had been a straw hat.
But you'll have all died long before that.

Exit. Enter SCEPARNIO, dragging a trunk in a net.

Sceparnio I never give up, me. How, you wonder, could
a little-known seaside slave ever hope to scrape together
enough money to buy himself? That's quite a lot of
money. Not a huge amount, but a bit, and a bit is much
more than not much even though it's not much. Quite
a lot is quite a lot, but much less than loads. Well the
answer is this. Us people of the sea, we pick things up.
The sea kind of mesmerises us, it's like a coin on a string
isn't it, swinging back and forth, it's like a big fat Father
Christmas in the shops going, come here little one, sit
on my knee, have you been a good boy? What do you
want for Christmas? Some ask for fish. Fair enough.
Some ask for foreign adventures, a wife in every port
and all that. Some ask for pearls. Some take a deep

breath and ask for sunken treasure. I'm one of them.
Well you know this coast is bristling with shipwrecks.
So you're sitting on the pier aged six with a bit of bacon
on the end of a string and you pull up a crab with a
Spaniard's boot in its grip. Oh all the world gets blown
to us. After that you can't work, you walk up and down
the beaches, eyes down, like bingo, hands behind your
back like Napoleon. Aha! A glint! Then you grow up
and get enslaved but you still do it every time you can,
it's a rollover every day down on the sand – but it's not
a lottery 'cause you don't have to pay. Oh everything's
free that comes out of the sea! And today I believe the
starry finger is pointing to me! I was joking just then,
I'm slave born. But inside me's the sea, that no one can
chain.

Takes the trunk out of the net.

So what have we got? Heavy, certainly. Somebody's
sodden laundry? A collection of back issues of Yellow
Pages?

He opens the trunk. He stands amazed.

This is – not – what – I – expected. This is – what – I
– dreamed. Mother! What king's been wrecked here?
Ancient? No. Modern. Help, who's looking? You keep
quiet about this, seagulls! This is me murdered if even
my grandmother sees! This is death, golden golden
strangulation. And there's a box within the box with –

He opens the casket inside the trunk.

A picture of a beautiful house. What? Never mind that.
I will wear him down, I will offer him ten times my
worth. Oh God, this is love, this is glory, this is freedom
surely!

Enter DAEMONES. SCEPARNIO hides.

Daemones Venus, you witch, when I had rid my mind
  Of wishes, you have got me wondering
  What love is like! It is that young man's passion,
  Dragging the pimp to jail, it is this flotsam,
  These dreamy mermaids sitting in my kitchen,
  Lost spirits of the ocean dancing foam,
  Heavy on land, translucent seahorses,
  Sipping their steaming char, too delicate
  To clean a teacup, let alone make the tea,
  Exhausted by the weight of their own beauty,
  Slumped on the table dazed and heavy-lidded,
  As with their dawn lit wave green eyes they stare
  Through the unending downpour of their hair.
  Useless for anything but – quite untrained
  Except in – . Just when I had rid my mind
  Of wishes, Venus gets me wondering!

He sees SCEPARNIO and the trunk.

  What's that you've got, shipmate?

Sceparnio Fish!

Daemones You've been out in this?

Sceparnio Sir, nothing stops me in my search for –

Daemones Sunken treasure?

Sceparnio And all I ever get is sea-creatures! If mackerel was
  a precious metal, if the prize for winning an International
  Football Championship was a sardine, if the bride and
  groom at their wedding exchanged gurnards, I would be
  rich! But it is not that kind of world.

Daemones No, it is not that kind of world. And what kind of
  fish is this?

Sceparnio Er – a trunkfish, sir.

Daemones Strange name! But it is a strange shape for a fish.

Sceparnio Not strange for a trunkfish.

Daemones I have never heard of this kind of fish.

Sceparnio Of course not! It doesn't exist! Not in the eyes of science! It has not been named yet. It's a creature of the profound deep, sir. It must have been washed up. Seven tenths of the world is water, sir. And only one millionth of that seven tenths has so far been explored!

Daemones Seven tenths of what you say is hogwash. But this must be worth a lot of money.

Sceparnio Oh no, not much.

Daemones No?

Sceparnio Well it's in terrible condition.

Daemones What are you going to do with it?

Sceparnio Chuck it back – after I've weighed it and measured it and got you to certify, sir, as a free man, that you witnessed it.

Daemones Well I'd better have a closer look at it.

Sceparnio Stop!

Daemones What?

Sceparnio It's highly explosive!

Daemones Explosive?

Sceparnio I was lying sir, it's not a fish it's a bomb. Look out! Boom!

He knocks DAEMONES over, and starts trying to drag off the trunk. DAEMONES gets up. SCEPARNIO throws himself to the ground, gets up, pretending to be dazed.

Sir, sir, are you all right?

Daemones Fine!

Sceparnio Better not return to it – you know, like fireworks –

Daemones Oh help! I think it's about to explode again! Boom!

Knocks SCEPARNIO down.

Sceparnio Thanks sir, you saved my life. Oh look out she's gonna blow again! Boom!

Knocks DAEMONES down.

Daemones Look out! Boom!

Knocks SCEPARNIO down. They abandon pretence and stand there knocking each other down, going boom! boom! Suddenly DAEMONES gets sick of it.

Stop it! You are my slave! Stop it!

Sceparnio Sorry sir.

Daemones Now what is this?

Sceparnio A trunk sir. There's nothing in it.

Daemones Good. I need an empty trunk. I'll take it.

Sceparnio No sir! I won't hear of it! Look, who's the master and who's the slave? Just help me get it up onto my back and I'll be off with it.

Daemones No, I feel like some exercise.

Sceparnio I won't hear of it!

Daemones I want to carry it!

Sceparnio I said no!

Daemones Why not?

Sceparnio Because you're a free man. I am a slave. I carry it.

Daemones Right. I will walk beside you. You will carry
it into the house, and there I will open it and see what's
inside it.

Sceparnio Nothing's inside it!

Daemones Good! I love nothing!

Sceparnio Oh sir please!

Daemones Please what?

Sceparnio All my life I've searched and searched – don't
take it away from me now at last I've found it!

Daemones An empty trunk?

Sceparnio Oh precious, precious emptiness! Think of that
trunk, sir, it contains freedom! Freedom from everything!
That's what emptiness is! Don't take away nothing from
me, sir!

Daemones I'm going to open it!

Sceparnio No! Then it will have something in it!

Daemones What?

Sceparnio Light! That's my darkness in there, I found it,
don't ruin it!

Daemones Shut up!

He opens the trunk.

Aha! Just what I thought! Treasure! So you wanted to
keep that from your master?

Sceparnio I found it!

Daemones But you are mine. What you find I own.

Sceparnio I need this money sir!

Daemones What for?

Sceparnio To buy my freedom! Sir, I will give you the whole trunk of money!

Daemones It is mine anyway. Perhaps I will start up in business again. No, no. Perhaps I will give it all to Venus. Now pick it up and carry it into the house. Sceparnio.

Sceparnio Yes sir.

Daemones I will set you free one day.

Sceparnio When? How old will I be?

Daemones I do not know the answer to that question.

Exit SCEPARNIO with trunk. Enter PALAESTRA.

Palaestra Hello.

Daemones Hello.

Palaestra How long will it take him?

Daemones Plesidippus? To get those enemies of mankind convicted? Not long, not long.

Palaestra Is he a nice man, do you think, Plesidippus?

Daemones Certainly a very nice man.

Palaestra I like him a lot.

Daemones Oh. You *like* him? Gotta do better than that if you're going to marry him.

Palaestra I can't do better than that.

Daemones Eh? Why not?

Palaestra I can't tell you why not.

Daemones Well it seems pretty clear to me.

Palaestra Oh yes?

Daemones It's because he's a besotted idiot.

M

O'
A
N
E
S
A S

MATELOTS

SUNDOWN

£1

Shakespeare's Globe

21 New Globe Walk
London
Tel: 0207 902 1500
VAT #: 494225090

DATE: 16 Oct 05 15:00:16
TRANSACTION REF: 1-0511-69519
SERVED BY: caitlin

	Sold	
JMBZ469	1	£6.74
The Storm		
INC. DISCOUNT OF	£2.25	

TOTAL	
SUB TOTAL	£6.74
VAT	£0.00
TOTAL	£6.74

TENDER	
Cash	£10.00
Change	£3.26

Palaestra An idiot to be besotted with me?

Daemones Well don't you want someone a bit more realistic? You, a woman of the street! Don't you want someone who doesn't go charging around getting his head bashed in by pimps, who doesn't spout romantic gibberish, someone who has shaken off some of his illusions, like you have? Someone disenchanted?

Palaestra I think my illusions could grow back overnight. I feel them sprouting like petunias all over the place.

Daemones Dangerous, dangerous! Life will come and stamp on them with giant feet!

Palaestra That sounds exciting.

Daemones It isn't. And Plesidippus will not be able to protect you from it. He is a clown.

Palaestra Who will then?

Daemones I don't know! Probably you need an older man. Think about it. With what you've been through, you must be several decades older than your actual age. Youth fades quick on the street. Your shell is pretty but inside you are an ancient crone, like a conker gone wrong, shiny outside and prickles within. You would be happiest, I would imagine, with someone washed up and hopeless like yourself.

Palaestra I'm torn.

Daemones Torn?

Palaestra Oh would you advise me!

Daemones I am not very good at giving advice. Look, am I a rich man?

Palaestra I don't care about that! You look wise to me!

Daemones That is just age. It is not the same thing.

Palaestra You're not that old!

Daemones But I'm not at all wise.

Palaestra Well I reckon –

Daemones What?

Palaestra You're quite bright if you know that. Take Labrax, now he really is thick. You can tell because he really thinks he's clever! If he was bright he'd be able to see through himself. But he can't. He could have a conversation with Socrates, and come away thinking, that bloke very nearly understood me.

Daemones Well you are rid of him.

Palaestra Yup! Goodbye to all that.

Daemones So will you change do you think, will you become respectable, when you marry Plesidippus, or will you run away to Spain and sleep with the matadors?

Palaestra I will change.

Daemones Good.

Palaestra But not all that much. I draw the line at morality. If I took on that, I wouldn't be able to earn my living. I ain't no steeplejack.

Daemones But you will be married.

Palaestra It won't last.

Daemones Why not?

Palaestra Coz I'm a tart. A tart at heart.

Daemones I do not believe that! You were not born a tart!

Palaestra True. It's only me outer shell that I sell.
The hearts about the only place the act of love does

not penetrate. Look, in my heart I'm Palaestra. But unfortunately I have lost control of my legs and my arms. No – I never had control of them! They were taken away from me before I knew what to do with them! My skin has gone wandering. Want to see what I mean?

Daemones I don't understand.

Palaestra Look!

She shows him a tattoo on her arse.

Daemones Diana?

Palaestra Yes! Haha! Diana, the chaste Goddess!

Daemones Why Diana?

Palaestra Come on! Where's the victory in having it away
with Venus? It's the celibate Goddess every man wants
to overpower. Chaste eh? We'll see about that!
And I run shrieking off into the forest,
With my nymphs sprinting, bows in hand, behind me,
Forming a screen to keep my white calves flashing
Beneath my buckskin skirt from male inspection!
Where the bee sucks and where the black bear rears
Erect, we race along the trails of beavers,
Fleeing, our cheeks bright red, our bosoms heaving,
Into the forest of virginity,
Away, away, among the female trees,
Where the bad wolf pants hotly in his passion
But not for us – away into the centre
Of the chaste forest, where a spring runs clear
Out of the coolness of the earth, and curves
Into a pool where we can see our beauties
Flat on the water till our diving stirs
The river's bed. Oh here no man will see us;
Here the perfection of our bodies equals
The glory of the water as it pours

Over the white rocks. What? I heard a twig snap!
What are you doing? Spying on the Goddess?
What are you doing in this forest, man,
You imperfection on the face of nature!
I am debased! Now see his knobbly antlers!

DAEMONES is beside himself.

Daemones You must drive all this out of your mind!

Palaestra Why?

Daemones It is not fair on a man! In the presence of a
prostitute – if she is beautiful and young and he is lonely
and not especially old and has learned nothing from a life
that is an indecipherable potsherd in his hand – then –

Palaestra Oh I see.

Daemones It's not fair on any man.

Palaestra Diana is waiting.

Daemones Shut up! Your name is Palaestra! Palaestra!
Palaestra!

Palaestra Too dangerous to be her. Too serious. I am Diana.

Daemones I do not have any money.

Palaestra Oh well nice talking to you anyway.

Daemones Actually I do! Quite a lot! I suddenly remember I
am rich, I am rich! Ask any price you want.

Palaestra There now, what was all that fuss about? We don't
need to talk anymore, do we? I will relieve you of all your
worries and most of your money…

Enter PTOLEMOCRATIA.

Ptolemocratia Ah, Mr Daemones!

Palaestra Goodbye!

Daemones Goodbye!

Exit PALAESTRA.

Ptolemocratia Mr Daemones – in my meditation
It came to me. I saw you saying nothing
Against the pimp, although your heart, I think
Cried out to you to free those women from him.
I saw you like a sailing boat the wind
Straining against the tide holds rigid and
To my surprise I found that I was crying.
Then Venus whispered in my ears, go to him,
He needs your help, he is a man steel-coffined
Inside a pyramid of lead. Go to him.
But you are glad now! We have freed the women.

Daemones I do not know what freedom is. Is freedom
Standing or moving, is it travelling
Or staying in one place? Is freedom freedom
From movement or from stasis or is freedom
Freedom from freedom? I suspect that freedom
Cancels out freedom so there is no freedom.

Ptolemocratia Nothing we do is worth a breath of time
If we are not enslaved to it by passion,
For sure. Without the chains of dedication,
Nothing we do can come to anything.
But these are abstract thoughts. There are two women
Who are no longer prostitutes. My Goddess
Rejoices and her carol makes an echo
In both our souls, I think.

Daemones   No, not in mine.

Ptolemocratia What did you say?

Daemones   Why can't they earn their living?

Ptolemocratia What do you mean?

Daemones   What do you think would happen
  If there were no tarts? On a Sunday evening,
  What would men do? Make plots against the empire,
  Or dance around a fire and strangle hamsters!

Ptolemocratia They do that anyway.

Daemones   They would do it more!
  The walls of Rome would shatter with frustration,
  And the whole empire would become a bonfire.

Ptolemocratia What would you say if it was your own daughter?

Daemones My daughter? What? Why do you mention her?

Ptolemocratia To melt your heart, and make you hate the power
  Of loveless love, which is an angel's grave!

Daemones Why do you have to speak about my daughter?
  Didn't you ever hear about the tower
  Whose base was smashed, but still the thing kept standing
  Proud as a soldier till the fact was mentioned?
  Haven't you ever heard about the castle
  Whose top half was built first, and the foundations
  Forgotten – it was tall, its top scraped heaven,
  But it was standing on a slab of nothing.

Ptolemocratia She was your rock.

  *DAEMONES goes downstage and addresses himself in
  different voices.*

Daemones   Now then, Mr Daemones,
  Would you just answer a few simple questions?
  Why do you think these men kidnapped your daughter?
  Because I was extremely rich. Aha –
  Was rich. I see. Why are you rich no longer?
  Because I gave it all away. You did
  What? I found out that gold is a false mirror –
  I made a heap and it made me a monster –
  I gave it all away to change the world,
  And change myself. And the world took your daughter!

You must have wished that you had kept back something!
A little million? Not at all! My reasons
Were sound! So you would make the same decision
Again? Yes! Lose your daughter to maintain
A principle? Of course! I mean of course not!
How can I? I will never make another
Decision in my life – the world can smother
In its own filth, I will not lift a finger!
The slightest act of kindness is disastrous!
So I am self-contained. I am in stasis.
That is impossible, Mr Daemones,
As Heraclitus said, all things are fire –
Even our bones, even these stones we stand on
Are hotly bursting out in all directions!
Even the sun climbs down from its convictions!
I am a solid flame! Impossible:
Change is the passion of the universe!
In which I have no part or patch or portion!
That is not possible, Mr Daemones –
The slightest act of kindness is disastrous –
So would you lose your daughter to maintain
A principle? Of course! I mean of course not!

He carries on in a loop that would last forever, but
PTOLEMOCRATIA gently sings over him till he stops:

Ptolemocratia Venus, fierce against all fences,
Weaver of coincidences,
Rouser of the heart's hot blood
When it rises in a flood
Out of clenched and trembling chambers;
To acquaint us with all strangers,
Rise out of the night and change us!
Let the beauty of the womb
Be a time bomb in the tomb;
With the power of the flocks
Crack the doors and smash the locks!
With an oak root break the cell,

73

With a tremor crack the shell
Of this man's ancestral hell!
Now come into the shrine with me and pray,
Neighbour, that she will break your chains this day!

Exeunt into the shrine.

Enter SCEPARNIO dressed as an old woman, dragging the trunk, which is covered in a cloth.

Sceparnio Hey! Hey! It's me! I know this doesn't suit me, I'm more an antique Roman than a dame. Actually I'm Greek of course. But I was prepared to sacrifice strict accuracy for the sake of the gag. In fact, I don't think there's anything I wouldn't sacrifice for the sake of a gag. Except for you my love!

Enter AMPELISCA, following him, her head covered.

Steady as we go, dear –

Ampelisca I'm not sure about this, Sceparnio –

Sceparnio Hush! Hush! Call me grandma! What did you say, my dear? Remember, remember, Ampelisca! If anyone asks, we are taking poor grandpa to bury him in Africa like he always wanted.

Ampelisca I'm not sure about this, grandma.

Sceparnio We're nearly away! Don't have second thoughts now, my pretty!

Ampelisca I can't help it.

Sceparnio I'm doing this for you! You said I had to be free!

Ampelisca You won't be a free man if you escape, you'll be a runaway slave. I'm sorry, grandma.

Sceparnio Please! I'll shower you with gold!

Ampelisca Not my idea of a good time.

Sceparnio I am a great lover! I practise all the time on my own!

Ampelisca Well you don't want to waste your genius on a worn-out tart from Cyrene. Let's be realistic, it will not be like the goddess of the moon stepping down out of the clouds. That's the trouble with you men: you look at the world through rose-tinted testicles.

Sceparnio Not me! Not any more: I've given up on the moon. I've waited for her too long! And the nymphs of the brooks and the dryads and the goddess of the frost, I have begged them on my bended knees but I can't get a thing out of them! Clapped-out tart suits me perfectly!

Ampelisca Look the main thing is I can't leave Palaestra.

Sceparnio Why are you so devoted to her?

Ampelisca Shall I tell you why? Will you try to understand? Once I tried to run away and do you know what they do to runaway slaves? They crucify them. Well while I was away to cover up for me she – stood in for me.

Sceparnio What do you mean?

Ampelisca She coped with all my clients as well as hers for three days till I came back shamefaced having got nowhere.

Sceparnio Oh my God.

Ampelisca So you see I couldn't possibly leave her after she put herself out like that for me.

Sceparnio She's got her love!

Ampelisca Who?

Sceparnio Plesidippus!

Ampelisca You don't get it do you. She won't marry him till she's found her father and she's got as much chance of doing that as I have of finding this coin again if I fling it into the sea!

She flings a coin into the audience and exits. SCEPARNIO goes down to the sea in despair.

Sceparnio Sea, my only teacher, I appeal to you, help me! These women are twisted! Not their fault, but. They are stuck, they are stuck! Slaves do not love, they breed. Sea! You are not that damp old man with a beard and a pitchfork, you are my maestro! Show me how to move her with storms! Oh dear – I see – if one day there are no slaves, there will still be those who are not free, and they will rage like me at the sea. Oh – what's that glittering in the water?

He gets audience to return coin, or 'finds' one behind someone's ear. Enter DAEMONES from the shrine. He dances with SCEPARNIO.

Daemones Venus has spoken! It has been arranged
In heaven! I have met my bride today!
Before the evening we will be united!
I do not know who Venus means! Her name
Will be revealed before the sun goes down!
But she already cuts through ropes, breaks chains,
Unmoors me from the wharf of memory!
The jailsprung blood runs shooting through my veins,
And I am eager for the mystery
To be revealed! Who will my sweetheart be?
What a pretty bonnet you are wearing, Sceparnio!

Sceparnio Sir, to celebrate, set me free!

Daemones Why?

Sceparnio Then we can have a double wedding! This woman is in love with me!

Daemones Are you?

Ampelisca Er – well – a bit.

Daemones A bit. You see! Again he jumps the gun!
Those who rush into things rush out again!

Sceparnio Yes sir.

Daemones Change cannot be avoided. We must grow
Monstrous if nothing else, that I do know,
Since I myself have suffered like a bulb
In my own frost for aeons. But I rise ·
Now to the light, because my spring has come.
If it was winter I would not be wise
To peep out yet. For me the ground is warm,
For you still white, so keep your green head down
My little primrose, or I'll punch your lights out. OK?

Sceparnio Priestess of Venus, intervene for me!

Ptolemocratia (*To DAEMONES.*) I think you ought to set this
young man free.

Daemones (*Not hearing.*) I am a convert to the creed of Venus.
I was an almost-atheist, a barrel
Of emptiness, a cracked and leaking ocean.
Now I am wine in a gold cup reflecting
The kindness of the sky and of the sea.
I am religious – how astonishing!
Here is the fire that burns inside of me!

Enter PALAESTRA.

(*Aside.*) Surely it must be her that Venus means?
How will I know?

Enter PLESIDIPPUS.

Plesidippus   Palaestra! Oh Palaestra!

Ptolemocratia Behold the husband!

Plesidippus   I have handed over
  Your owner to the fury of the law.
  Your former owner, I should say – no more
  Entitled to you now than fish to air!
  Now you are mine! I publicly declare
  To all you people here, my dedication,
  As long as I have life, to this one woman,
  To care for her, to help and shelter her,
  To drive all demons far away from her,
  By brandishing the furious torch of passion
  That turns all shadows into sunflowers!

Sceparnio May I just say that it was me who found her –

Plesidippus (*Ignoring SCEPARNIO.*) Give me your hand.

Palaestra   There is one tiny problem.

Plesidippus What?

Palaestra   When I was sixteen I made a vow
  That I would not allow myself to fall
  In love till I had found my father. Listen:
  You are in all respects a perfect man,
  But I cannot betray the tearful girl
  Who made that promise to herself. I'm sorry.

Daemones I think you'll have to find him.

Sceparnio As I just told you, it was me who found her,
  And if you want to thank me, ask my master
  To set me free.

Daemones   I cannot set you free,
  I do not think it would be good for me.

Sceparnio But sir if you do not free me Ampelisca will not
  marry me. Will you?

Ampelisca No.

Sceparnio And you won't marry me unless Palaestra is married, will you?

Ampelisca No.

Sceparnio I will fling myself off the cliff! I will commit seaside!

Daemones You can't do that! You are my property!
Look – you have pushed me into a decision –
Yes! But there are two ifs before the purchase:
If this young woman finds her father and
Marries this young man, if these two things happen,
Then I will give you what this trunk contains,
So that you can invest it in your freedom,
Buy yourself off me. Happy now, Sceparnio?

Sceparnio Oh so happy! All I have to do is find this father of all things!

Enter CHARMIDES.

Plesidippus What are you doing out of jail, you vampire? Where is your friend?

CHARMIDES is wearing LABRAX's hat, through which there is a bullet hole. He takes it off and fingers it.

Charmides   My friend was not my friend.
He thought I was, but he was wrong, quite wrong.
I am the man that he was running from.
Like in the Usual Suspects.

Plesidippus   Eh?

Charmides   You haven't
Seen it? You haven't lived, you haven't breathed,
You antique crowd of backward theatregoers.
I am the man most simply known as *him*.
I have inherited the property
Of Labrax, owner of these two young women.

Plesidippus You should be locked up!

Charmides   Yes I should. But sadly
  Something has happened.

Plesidippus   Why are you not crushed
  Under the hobnailed sandal of the Empire?
  You broke the law! How can the wolf mother
  Not guzzle on your guts? Is there no justice?

Charmides An accident has happened to the law.

Plesidippus What do you mean? What can affect the law?
  Can the law cut its finger on a saw?
  Fall off a log and dislocate its jaw?
  Get its foot stuck in a revolving door?

Charmides Something even worse than these rhymes has
  happened, sir.

Plesidippus What? Tell us! Tell us! Spit it out for God's sake!

  CHARMIDES removes his hat.

Charmides Rome has been captured by the Goths. I'm sorry.

Daemones Rome has not fallen!

Charmides   Like the leaves of autumn,
  Sadly.

Daemones But how on earth can it have happened?

Charmides Too wide an empire and too tight a margin,
  Too many proud lords too loud to listen;
  Many tall stories, many a short temper,
  That was the end of the Roman Empire.
  Pity. It wasn't clever or funny,
  But it was a licence to print money.

Sceparnio Freedom!

Charmides With the result that these two girls are mine,
  Citizens or not citizens. I paid

80

Money for them, and money is a law
Unto itself, it needs no Lex Romana!

Ptolemocratia You shall not steal their souls!

Charmides   Of course not, madam.
When push comes to shove and shove comes to push,
It's their muffs I want, I'm not beating about the bush.

Ptolemocratia Venus!

Charmides Madam, if you examine your conscience, you
will find that I am not to blame.

Ptolemocratia Sir, if you examine your conscience, you will
find that you have not got one.

Plesidippus Wait! I paid half the money, didn't I?
That was the sum you squandered on the sea
When your boat sank! That was my up-front payment
For a star's light, compared to which perfection
Is crassness! And you ran away with it!
Not your first crime! But I will overlook it,
If you can now achieve a change of heart,
Act like a businessman for once, complete
The deal we struck, hand over this young woman
For the agreed sum! If you will not do that,
Then we will have to fight! What is your verdict?

Charmides Gentlemen, Ladies, I am in mourning for the
classical period, I don't want to make a fuss. Let us not
start this new epoch off on the wrong foot, or it could
turn out to be a terribly dark age. Yes, I renounce my
twisty instincts! From now on I am a brasso'd bed knob,
squeaky clean, like a shampoo'd mouse. Pay me the rest
you owe for her, and she's yours, and look – no fingers
crossed.

Plesidippus I have the money on me… Oh! It's gone!

81

Charmides (*Aside.*) Swiped it off him on the beach when we thought he was dead. Oh well, come on girls! A beautiful relationship that was not to be. Now, don't give us any trouble, Mr Plesidippus, I am a civilized man, but if provoked I am a psychotic killer.

Sceparnio Stop!

Charmides Yes?

Sceparnio My master is a rich man! He can buy them!

Plesidippus But will he though? Will he do anything, Ever? He is determined to do nothing!

Daemones That's true. So if you try to take this trunk full of money off me, I can't do anything to stop you.

After a moment PLESIDIPPUS twigs, and goes to the trunk.

Sceparnio Palaestra! Now he can marry you!

Palaestra Yes!

Plesidippus / Sceparnio Thank God!

Palaestra When he finds my father!

Plesidippus / Sceparnio Aaaggghhhh!!

Charmides Wonderful! You have found my trunk! Oh thank you!

Uncovers the trunk. PALAESTRA gasps.

Sceparnio Yours?

Charmides Yes!

Sceparnio Prove it! What's in it?

Charmides Lots of money!

Sceparnio Yes! And?

Charmides (*With mock effort.*) Oh – um – er – a casket, yes, a
    casket!

Sceparnio Lucky guess. Ah, but what's in the casket?

Charmides I don't know! It's her casket, isn't it!

Daemones I know that casket.

Sceparnio Palaestra, you've never seen this casket have you?

    PALAESTRA is silent.

Ptolemocratia Palaestra, what's in the casket?

Daemones Say what is in the casket!

Palaestra I will keep nothing back, I will recite
    The contents of the casket of my heart.
    It is a simple picture of a house.
    I am aware that it's no masterpiece,
    But it is not for its artistic merit
    That I adore it. You may call it foolish
    To lift your soul down off its shelf of flesh
    And put it in a box where you can lose it.
    But it was far more likely to be lost
    In my hot hands than locked in this cold casket.
    Or so I thought! But then the sea's fish mouth
    Pouted, and down it slipped into its gullet –
    Where I presumed it would have been digested,
    Or broken by the squabbling ghosts of pirates –
    And for a while I was without my soul,
    Like a glass bowl without a golden fish.

Daemones May I see it? May I see it?

Palaestra You want to see my soul? Well I am flattered.
    But it is mine, you will not recognise it.
    A picture of the house where I was born
    Is what it is. The men who stole me from
    My father took this too and it has followed
    My body over seas and over countries

Somehow, as if it was a dog whose name
Only I know, so I know I am I
By its obedience. This house is magic.
It is my home. I hide behind the curtains.

DAEMONES looks at the picture in amazement, delight and horror.

Daemones Diana?

Palaestra Have a quick look! My soul is in the open!
Everyone take a peek before I pop it
Back in box until the next millennium.

Daemones Diana! I have found you! My Diana!

Palaestra Well mister if you want me, find the money.

Daemones You are my daughter!

Palaestra   That will cost you extra.

Daemones It is my daughter!

Palaestra Your daughter?

Daemones It is our old house – Villa Croesus. My little one. My giggler.

He weeps in PTOLEMOCRATIA's arms. She notices his tears.

Ampelisca If he recognises the house, Palaestra, he must be your father.

Palaestra Don't talk soft, he's just a pervert – it says the name on the back.

Ampelisca Does it?

Palaestra Course it does! What's he take me for – (*Looks at it.*) Oh, where's the name gone?

Ampelisca Washed off in the sea!

Palaestra (*Aside.*) Christ, I nearly did it with my dad! I've got to get out of this business.

Charmides Which proves the trunk is mine.

Daemones Take it then!

Plesidippus Yes take it! Money is the death of love!
Passion can only thrive in poverty!
Is that not right my love?

Palaestra I wouldn't know.

Charmides And the girls, since you can't pay for them!

Sceparnio You won't take them!

*CHARMIDES, with the girls in his grip, pulls out a gun.
Everyone freezes.*

Daemones Nothing to be done. Ah! There is a gun in the house!

*He runs out and re-enters with the gun pointed at
CHARMIDES.*

Let go of the girls!

Charmides So you can get a clear shot?

Daemones Demon!

Charmides Twat!

DAEMONES puts down his gun.

Daemones I can't shoot him.

Charmides But I can shoot you.

*He is about to shoot DAEMONES when PTOLEMOCRATIA
leaps on him and they stagger to the front of the stage, wrestling
over the gun. Freeze.*

Sceparnio Ladies and gentlemen, we are very sorry, but we forgot to mention that there will be one gunshot during this performance.

The gun falls into the audience. The girls start to move towards DAEMONES...but CHARMIDES draws a knife and gets them back. SCEPARNIO picks up the gun DAEMONES has dropped. He points it at CHARMIDES.

Charmides If that's the gun from Act One it's been in the sea for six hours, I don't think it'll be wildly accurate.

Sceparnio True. Damn. What a twat I am.

He puts the gun to his head carelessly and pulls the trigger. It goes off. The girls scream. DAEMONES rushes up to him.

Daemones It's alright! It went straight through without hitting anything!

Ampelisca / Palaestra But – look – what –

They point to where a dead STEWARD is being carried out of the auditorium.

Palaestra You've shot one of the stewards!

Daemones Speak to me, speak to me boy!

Sceparnio Free. I am free. No wishes. I am empty.
No fears. I am a sky with no horizon,
A fish free-floating out of school, bound homewards,
Into the air, a leaf in love with falling.

Daemones Oh no!

Ptolemocratia Has he lost his mind?

Daemones Much worse! I'm afraid he's gone into verse.

CHARMIDES starts to escape with the girls.

Ampelisca Sceparnio!

86

Sceparnio What? Who?

PLESIDIPPUS picks up the gun and points it at CHARMIDES.

Charmides Oh no!

He puts the knife to PALAESTRA's throat. Stalemate.

Palaestra Since we are stuck like this, I might point out that
nobody's asked us what we want. Or who we want. (*To
PLESIDIPPUS.*) Have they, my sweetheart?
This man will beat me, cheat me, wear me down,
But he will never *let* me down, because he
Will never set me up. What kind of life
Does a wife have? If I work hard, I reckon
I'll be the Chairman of the company
Of my own body in a year or two –
But as a wife I'll always be the doorman.
Too much like hard work. So – to Barcelona!
Where I'll lie down, switch off my head, and earn.
We had no idea, Charmides, that you were *him*. If only
you'd told us that in the beginning! (*To the others.*) You
can forget us, riff raff! We're going with *him*. This way
(*Towards the cliff.*) is quickest.

Daemones   Stop, Diana! Stop!

Plesidippus Your father has been found, my love!

Palaestra   He has.
And what a father. What a dirtbag. God!
He tried to pay me for it! See yer, dad.

Ampelisca I'm going too. Where she goes I go. Sorry.

Daemones Stop! The cliff, you lunatic!

*She leads CHARMIDES to the weak part of the cliff. She
skips around it, he falls, screaming, with the trunk. All
grab onto the trunk (except SCEPARNIO, who is floating*

87

around in a state of bliss). CHARMIDES is hanging on for dear life.

Charmides Palaestra! I love you!

Daemones Don't let go of the money!

He, PLESIDIPPUS, PTOLEMOCRATIA and AMPELISCA bunch up, pulling at the trunk. DAEMONES is behind PTOLEMOCRATIA.

Venus! I understand now who you had in mind for me!

Charmides No! Please! I'll be a nun!

Enter VENUS from above.

Venus Children, your goddess from above
Has come to save you with her love.

Daemones Venus? But Rome's dead, there's different gods now!

Venus Oh, so I don't exist?

Shrugs and re-ascends.

Daemones Sceparnio! Help us! This is your money, remember, now she's found me; you need it to buy yourself off me!

Charmides Mr Daemones, you are my mentor, you've taught me everything I know, I look up to you! And to pay you back, I want to give you half this money if you'll come into partnership with me. Mr Daemones – the Roman Empire is dead, let's replace it with a business empire of our own; don't tell me your genius has fallen asleep, Mr Daemones! Think what we could do!

Daemones Must be a lot of roofs off after the storm. Buy up all the thatch in Greece! Must be a lot of ships

down. Get into shipping quick! What else? A chain of
whorehouses, starting in Barcelona! Heave, Sceparnio!

Sceparnio I do not think it would be good for you.

*SCEPARNIO kicks away the hand holding the trunk.
CHARMIDES falls with a long drawn-out scream.*

(*With contempt.*) Money!

Daemones Sceparnio!

*PALAESTRA goes over to PLESIDIPPUS, who is sitting
with his head in his hands.*

Plesidippus Well it is true. I cannot say for certain
That I would treat you better than your owner,
My love could be no less tyrannical,
And for the profit of my satisfaction,
Enslave you like a baby with its hunger.

Ptolemocratia There is no safe love. Look how sick he is.
No prophylactic for the heart, is there?
No sheath to keep the spirit from contracting
Devotion, and this man is riddled with it.

Plesidippus Palaestra!

Palaestra   I am not, it seems, Palaestra.
I am Diana. That is what my father
Named me, and what I named myself, not knowing,
For purposes of commerce. But it is
A good name, I will take it back again,
And suit it better, if my life allows me.

Plesidippus It was not me who found your father, but –

Palaestra He has been found, and you will be my husband,
But not yet. Priestess, do you love my father?

Ptolemocratia Yes, in fulfilment of the prophecy
Of Venus.

Palaestra   Then resign from your position,
   And be his wife, and make a good man of him,
   And let me be the priestess at this shrine,
   Whichever God it will belong to now,
   For who knows how long. Till my former life,
   Too salty, has dissolved into the ocean
   With that bad man. This is a better one,
   Though he knows all about my working life,
   All my brief husbands who have come and gone
   Quicker than blowflies on a leg of gammon,
   He loves me. When I've finished with religion,
   If he still wants me he will be my husband,
   But not before that!

Plesidippus   I accept my sentence!
   And I will come with flowers every morning,
   Offerings for the goddess. I will sing
   Hymns to her Highness all night long, eat seaweed,
   Sleep on the rocks, till I become your husband!

Daemones (*To PTOLEMOCRATIA.*) Surely you can see
   through me?

Ptolemocratia I can. Any woman can see through any man.
   But luckily the universe is comprised of equal parts of
   matter and doesn't matter.

Palaestra So Rome is over. No more roads and togas.
   What will come next? Perhaps the gods we know
   Will disappear. A pity, I did like them.
   Venus could not prevent my prostitution,
   But she did save me. What I say is this:
   If any other goddess takes her place
   Who does not help the working girls, God help her.
   As for myself, now that the coast is clear,
   I have a life to jettison, a thousand
   Coats to throw off before it is my own
   That I am standing in, at the beginning.

Daemones (*To PALAESTRA.*) I am sorry.

Palaestra So am I.

They embrace.

> Oh my poor father, have to just forgive you
> For not being Apollo, and remember
> That you and I would both have been immortal
> If we had not been parted.

Daemones   My dear daughter.

Sceparnio (*Looking over the cliff.*) The pimp! He's survived!
He's running down the beach! Oh! Look! A giant crab
has crawled out of the sea! Its grabbed Charmides in
one claw! Oh! It's pulled off his head! Now it's bitten
him in half! Oh! Horrible! How could it do that? They'll
eat anything, those crustaceans! Oh good, I'm back to
prose again.

Palaestra Aren't you going to free this man?

Sceparnio Sir, don't! If she won't love me as a slave she
won't love me free! If she can't freely love me as a slave,
she can't love me, if you see what I mean. Or maybe she
could, well probably she would, but you know, then I
would just be happy.

Daemones (*To AMPELISCA.*) If you wish to, you can marry
my slave.

Ampelisca I do wish to.

Daemones And since I am a poor man, I have nothing to
give you for a wedding present except for – his freedom.

Sceparnio Free love!

They dance and sing:

All Over and over again they fly
Out of the earth into the sky,

PETER OSWALD

Why do they shine so brightly, why?
The flowers of spring, the flowers of spring!

What's the religion of a rose?
God only knows, God only knows!
Its church is old, its priests are crows,
The flowers of spring, the flowers of spring!

Why is the sea so deep and wide?
What does a blue whale hold inside?
A Himalayan mountainside?
The flowers of spring, the flowers of spring!

Night will descend with chains of wool,
Stars will let down silk ropes to pull,
And every buttercup will be full,
The flowers of spring, the flowers of spring!

Exeunt.

Enter the WEATHER, who speaks or sings:

Weather Now you've heard the wild wind
Of an old tale refined
In a right Roman mind,
And passed on down the line.
A modern impression
Of the oldest profession,
And a bewildering history lesson.
I wish you fair sailing
Without too much bailing,
Hearts light as a feather
In heavenly weather!

End.